Building Si

CW01604203

A Cherrytree Book

Designed and produced by
A S Publishing

First published 1989
by Cherrytree Press Ltd
a subsidiary of
The Chivers Company Ltd
Windsor Bridge Road
Bath, Avon BA2 3AX

British Library Cataloguing in Publication Data

Amos, Janine
To a building site.
1. Building. Construction. Sites. For children
I. Title II. Reed, Neil
III. Series
690

ISBN 0 7451 5072 1

Printed in Italy by Imago Publishing Ltd

Let's go to a

Building Site

By Janine Amos
Illustrated by Neil Reed

CHERRYTREE BOOKS

In the country, buildings are far apart. In towns they are close together. There is not much room for houses. Many people live in flats. Let's go to a building site and see a new block of flats being built.

Before the builders start, the land for the flats has to be checked. An engineer makes sure that the land is all right to build on. He tests the soil and drills down to see that the rock below is firm. A surveyor measures the size, shape and height of the land.

The surveyor measures the land with special instruments. One instrument is called a level. It measures differences in the level of the ground.

The surveyor makes a plan of the site. It shows where trees, drains and other buildings are.

He gives the plan to the architect. The architect designs the building. This architect has designed a block of flats with eight storeys.

The architect makes detailed drawings that show the shape of the building. She decides what kind of stone or concrete to make the walls from. She chooses what wood or metal to use.

An engineer checks that the building will stand up. The developer works out how much it will cost.

Buildings do not stand on top of the land. They go right down into the ground. The part of the building below ground is called its foundations. The foundations are made of concrete.

Tall buildings stand on piles. These are pillars of concrete and steel. A machine called a pile driver hammers the piles into the ground.

Earth and rubble are removed from the site by excavators and lorries.

The site manager is in charge. He makes sure that all the building materials are ready. He makes sure that the builders finish the work on time. He shows us round the site. He gives us a Fact File that answers lots of questions.

The builders make a frame for the flats. It is like the skeleton in your body. It will hold the building up.

Metal rods are placed into a mould made of wood and steel. Liquid concrete is poured in. The rods make the concrete stronger. It is called reinforced concrete.

The frame is built up floor by floor.

As it gets higher, the builders put up scaffolding. Scaffolding is made of metal poles bolted together.

The builders put wooden planks across the poles. They stand on the planks to work.

Cranes lift heavy loads around the site. Later they will hoist the stairs and the lift into the building.

walls

The outer walls of the flats are to be made of bricks.
The brick walls are lined with thick concrete blocks.
The blocks and the bricks are stuck together with mortar.
Mortar is a mixture of cement, sand and water.

The bricklayer takes special care that the walls are level.

damp proofing

Damp from the ground may rise up through bricks and make them wet. The building must be protected from this damp. The site manager explains how it is done.

After the first few rows of bricks, a layer of waterproof material made from tar is laid down. This keeps the walls dry. The stony floor is covered with a smooth layer of sand. Then a big sheet of thick polythene is laid over it. A layer of concrete goes on top. No damp can creep through it.

The floors of the building are made of concrete blocks. They are laid between the concrete beams. The concrete floor is covered by a layer of foam. This keeps the cold out. It keeps out sound, too. The people who live in the flats will be nice and warm. They will not hear each other moving about. A smooth concrete floor is laid on top of the foam.

Working high on the scaffolding is dangerous. It is dangerous down below, too. Everyone on the site must wear a hard hat to protect his head.

Water, gas and electricity are brought to the flats in underground pipes. The pipes are laid in trenches. The trench sides are supported with metal props.

windows

The builders know from the plans where each door and window is to go. The window frames are delivered to the site ready-made. The frames are propped in position with planks. The bricklayers work round them.

A steel beam called a lintel is placed above each window and door. This holds up the bricks above.

Down on the ground, spaces have been left for the pipes to enter the flats.

pipes and cables

The site manager is pleased. All the work is running to time. The outer walls are built. All the floors are in. The stairs have been built. Now it is time for the roof to go on.

We watch as huge lorries arrive. They are carrying some great big pieces of wood. They are joined together in V shapes. These are the roof trusses.

A crane lifts the trusses to the top of the scaffolding.

The builders fix them to the concrete beams at the top of the frame. The trusses are covered with a layer of roofing felt. This is a thick waterproof material. Long pieces of wood called battens are nailed on top.

The site manager explains how the roof is tiled. The concrete tiles are nailed on the battens. Each tile has two hooks on it, called nibs. These slip over the batten so that the tile hangs in place. Each new row of tiles overlaps the last.

The roof is built at an angle. Rainwater runs down it. The builders fix plastic gutters all round the roof. The rainwater runs into them. Drain-pipes lead from the gutters to the ground. The water goes into underground drains and is carried away.

first fixing

The building is now ready for its 'first fixing'. Glass panes are put into the window frames. They are fixed in with a kind of clay called putty. It is like plasticine except that it dries hard.

Electricians fix the main electricity cables in place.

The inside walls are lined with big boards of smooth plaster. These sheets of plasterboard are cemented to the blocks. This is called dry-lining.

Thicker panels of plasterboard are used to divide each flat into separate rooms.

second fixing

Now the electricians and carpenters begin the next stage of work. It is called the 'second fixing'.

Each room needs lights and plugs. An electrician fits them. The bathroom and kitchen need pipes, taps, sinks, a lavatory and a bath. The plumber fits those. A heating engineer puts in the central heating. There are radiators in every room.

Now the flats are beginning to look like homes.

There is still a lot to do. The site manager calls in the decorators. All the ceilings and walls are smoothed. Then they are painted. The painters put on two layers of paint.

When the painters have finished, carpets will be laid.

The walls of the kitchens and bathrooms are tiled. A carpenter fits a door into each room. He makes sure that all the doors open and close properly.

The site manager inspects everything. Each job has to be done well.

Outside, all the big machines have gone. The building materials and rubble have been cleared away. The drain trenches have been covered over again. The woodwork has been painted. A path is laid that leads to the front entrance. A car park is made at the back.

The architect inspects the building with the site manager. They are both very pleased with it. So are we. So are the people who are going to live there.

the finished building

Fact File

What are buildings made of?
Building materials can be wood, stone, steel, bricks or even glass. Most buildings are made of some type of stone. Crushed stone is used to make concrete. Most modern buildings are made of steel and concrete. Reinforced concrete is made extra strong with rods of steel.

Do all buildings have a frame?
Even a hut needs a frame! The frame is the bones of the building. It bears the weight of the roof and the walls.

What are frames made of?
Frames are made of columns, beams and girders. They can be made of wood, metal or reinforced concrete. Columns are tall upright supports. Girders are supports that go across. Beams are small girders.

Do all buildings have foundations?
Foundations are very important. You can only build something heavy on a firm base. If you built on sand, your building would sink

The Sears Tower makes ordinary buildings look very small

into it. If you built on solid rock, with no foundations, the building would move. Even a path has foundations.

How high can you build a building?
All the time, people are trying to build higher buildings. The Sears Tower in the United States is the world's tallest building. It has 110 storeys.

How long do buildings last?
Buildings made from stone can last for thousands of years. The pyramids in Egypt were built over 4000 years ago. Even wooden buildings can last for hundreds of years.

Why are buildings made of wood?
People make buildings of wood in countries where there are lots of forests and not much stone. Wooden houses usually have very steep roofs. The snow slides off them. They have extra-thick walls. They keep the cold out and the heat in.

What kinds of houses do people build in rainy places?
When it rains a lot, the ground gets wet and boggy. Houses have to be built on stilts, high above the wet ground.

Can anyone build a house where they like?
In most countries, you have to get permission before you build a house. Even if you own the land, the design of your building has to be approved. It must look right and fit in with other houses round about. It must also be safe and fire-proof.

Index